Water

CASSIE MOORE

WordPower Book Series

For more information, contact:

Fig Factor Media, LLC | www.figfactormedia.com

Cover Design & Layout by Juan Pablo Ruiz
Printed in the United States of America

ISBN: 978-1-959989-55-4

DEDICATION

To my husband and best friend Mark, who supports my endeavors with love, kindness, patience, and a good dose of humor. He has enriched my life at every turn.

ACKNOWLEDGMENTS

I would like to acknowledge Fig Factor Media for this opportunity to express my creative talents. Karen Dix, who led me to this project and encouraged me to take the leap of action.

To my children, Bill and Chelsea, who have been my greatest teachers in life. They continually inspire me to be a better version of myself.

To my darling little nuggets, Liam and Brooke, who have awoken a renewed sense of joy at life's simplest treasures.

My sisters, Margaret and Mary, who encouraged and inspired me to challenge myself. Your feedback and comments were invaluable to this process.

My parents, Art and Jackie, who had a love of nature and a willingness to provide us with our endless summers on Big Twin Lake in northern Wisconsin. It was the backdrop to my love and devotion to water and nature.

INTRO

Water is the essence of life. It is essential to every living organism. I am intrinsically connected to water.

I recently discovered I have a Blue Mind. A Blue Mind is the term used to describe the state of water-associated peace. Scientists worldwide have studied the numerous positive effects of water. Combining cutting-edge neuroscience and compelling data, Professor Michael DePledge of Oxford University and England's Chief Scientist of the Environmental Agency, observes that people living near coastlines, or any blue space, are happier, healthier, more connected, and live longer lives. Blue-Minded people are generally more successful, across the board.

Join me as I explore the wisdom and joy found in water, and its intricate role in our lives. I have visited countless beaches in my travels, and they have all grounded me in self-discovery. How does water play a role in your life? Read on and you may discover you have a Blue Mind.

TRANQUILITY

I am sitting on the end of our pier, dangling my toes in the water. I am in northern Wisconsin on a secluded, crystal-clear lake. I tiptoed down to the pier when the first rays of sun were bursting over the horizon. The fog is lifting, as the sun warms the surface of the water. This is heaven. I breathe deeply and think how grateful I am to be in this moment, to witness God's beautiful handiwork. I am calm and more at peace next to these tranquil waters than in any other place. I am at my best. My soul sings in gratitude with complete solitude and harmony.

The loon starts his morning call as I realize I have company in this beautiful, serene moment when light fills the darkness. I am content, resting by still waters. It is a tranquil pool.

It is during this time that my heart and mind align as I meditate. I have clarity of thought only produced by the stillness. I feel empowered and balanced. I have found my home in nature.

"No one can see their reflection in running water; it is only in still water we can see." -TAOIST PROVERB

FLOW

The flow of water teaches us to let go and move forward, embracing the flow of life. Letting go may be one of the hardest things to accomplish. It takes courage and determination. Letting go is a myriad of different meanings for everyone. It is the big unknown, with lots of uncertainty. However, it can make a world of difference in the outcome of your life. Doing what feels authentically 'you' and genuinely right sets you on path to letting go of everything else.

A river flows, it changes, progresses and unfolds. Moving water has a fascinating vitality. When you let the mind flow like water, it opens itself to change and unending possibilities.

Live your life like a river. Embrace the flow of life. Let go of things that no longer serve your greater purpose. Create a new path, washing away things that are negative influences. Sit quietly within yourself and let your mind flow like water. Allow the current to lead you to a new a refreshing outlook.

"Rivers know this: there is no hurry. We shall get there some day."
-A.A. MILNE-

RESTORE AND REPLENISH

Water restores and replenishes. Water is the soul of the earth. Even the earth rejoices after a soaking spring rain. The musky, earthy smell reinvigorates and promises renewal and growth.

Respect your need to rest. When you take the time to replenish your spirit, it allows you to pull from reserves. In today's world we push ourselves to the point of exhaustion. Our society equates busy with success. Burnout is real, and it can have major consequences. It can leave you empty, discouraged and exhausted, with little energy for much else. We need to pause, rest, refresh, and restore.

Water provides the beautiful ability to reset all our senses. Such as a delicious cool glass of water, a warm soak in a bathtub restoring our aching muscles. Perhaps, staring out over the water, listening to the gentle lapping of waves. Be intentional and take the time to be still. Let water wash over you.

"When I sit here by the sea and listen to the sound of the waves, I feel free from all obligations and people of this world."
-HENRY DAVID THOREAU-

Cassie Moon

STRENGTH

Water is a force to be reckoned with. Its strength is unyielding. It can have fearsome effects in the erosion of anything in its path.

I stood by Niagara Falls several years ago and was terrified. It took my breath away. The sheer power and volume of water was indescribable. I couldn't bring myself to walk close to the railing. I was in awe and rapture of this incredible force of nature, only feet from where I was standing. I will never forget the emotional response I felt to my core, being a mere speck next to this giant. It was humbling.

The ocean embodies strength in its vastness—soft and fluid or powerful and unyielding. We too can draw strength from resources deep within ourselves. We find our strength through hidden reserves of courage and resilience. It is extraordinary, the amount of resilience in human nature. No one can take away our inner strength. Bring your hidden strength forward, it is the greatest gift you can give yourself.

"I can be changed by what happens to me. But I refuse to be reduced by it."
-MAYA ANGELOU-

PURIFICATION

The value of water to human existence extends well beyond its life-sustaining properties. Water purifies your mind, body, and soul. Water's dynamic capacities are recognized and revered by spiritual traditions across cultures. It provides emotional balance and happiness. Most faiths give great reverence to the sacredness of water, as seen in many traditional purification rites.

Drinking a glass of water purifies our insides, it supports our tissues and organs. It is the essence of our body's function. Nearly all your body's major systems depend on water to function and survive. Water purifies and renews, it's the essence of life.

Just like a warm spring rain shower, water cleanses, refreshes, and purifies. It brightens our senses. The earth smells fresh and clean. Like the rain, cleansing your mind clears out the old and washes it anew. Purifying our thoughts removes the congestion and clutter we carry in our mind. Life will align when you embrace and free your mind from stagnant thoughts.

"Body is purified by water, self is purified by tears, intellect is purified by knowledge, and the soul is purified with love." -IMAM ALI-

CONNECTEDNESS

Water connects us as a human race. Water is essential to all life here on Earth. Every culture moves towards water. It is what connects us as people. Just like raindrops, we, as individuals, make up one ocean.

We connect to other people in a common shared human experience. Every single person has an extraordinary story. We may believe that we have unremarkable lives. What we share is our human experience. We have all done something that is fascinating, that took courage, that is difficult, and something we should be proud of. Everyone has a story to tell.

It is our collective consciousness as humans that connects us to each other. One raindrop may be an individual contribution, but together we make up an absolute whole, kindred spirits on a journey called life.

"As many raindrops join to form a great river of water, many souls join their highest intent to form the river of evolved consciousness."
-JONATHON LOCKWOOD HUIE-

PEBBLES IN WATER

I am standing on the shoreline with my three-year-old grandson, Liam. We are tossing pebbles into the lake. He is squealing with delight at the splashes. We watch the ripples flow out into endless circles towards distant shorelines.

Words, just like the ripples in the water, travel out to endless destinations. Their impact reaches destinations we can only imagine. I look down into his innocent face as he starts this journey on earth and wonder what words will impact his life. His mind is a fertile ground, like a little sponge. Words will mold and shape him, defining his character.

Words are powerful. They have the power to inspire, encourage, and heal. However, they can also hurt, destroy, humiliate, and reject. One word can make the difference. Guard your words. Their impact can be far reaching, just like the ripples in the water. They create images and memories that can last a lifetime. Be wise, enrich, and bless with your words.

"Kind words are a creative force, a power that concurs in the building up of all that is good and energy that showers blessings upon the world."
-LAWRENCE G. LOVASIK-

ADAPTABILITY

I am standing on the banks of the Brule River, Wisconsin, watching its movement. It's flexible; it adapts to the landscape; it twists and turns. The water flows over obstacles; it seeps through cracks and crevices. It is fluid and adaptable.

Much like the river, water in any container adapts to the shape of the vessel in which it is contained. Be flexible.

Change is inevitable, it is an ongoing reality in our lives. When we embrace this fact, we allow ourselves the freedom to be open to infinite possibilities. The more fluid you are, the more alive you are. It allows creativity to flow, because you are not exhausting yourself by swimming upstream against the rapids of change. Adapt to your surroundings. Do not stay rigid in your thinking. There is wisdom in watching water flow.

"Empty your mind, be formless. Shapeless like water. If you put water into a cup, it becomes the cup. You put water into a bottle it becomes the bottle. Now water can flow, or it can crash. Be water my friend."
-BRUCE LEE-

NATURES SYMPHONY

Music fills my soul with joy, letting the notes take me on a journey through my memories, evoking images from my past. It can change your mood and enlighten your thoughts. It can inspire or bring you to tears. Music can transform any moment in our lives.

Nature orchestrates its own symphony of sound, especially the sounds of water—the soft babbling of a brook, the sound of rain on the roof, the gentle lapping of waves as they cascade towards the shore.

It plays on my soul like a soothing balm. It restores my spirit; it commands my attention. It restores the rhythm of my life with clarity and holds infinite potential. The sounds inspire me to align with my purpose in life. Its deep notes play a song that leads my mind to connect with nature. Water's sound is limitless in its changing crescendos, never playing the same concert twice. It is infinite. We are its audience.

"They both listened silently to the water, which to them was not just water, but the voice of life, the voice of Being, the voice of perpetual Becoming."
-HERMANN HESSE-

SMALL THINGS, BIG IMPACT

The tiniest stream of water can cut and burrow its way through the hardest landscape. One drop of water may not seem like a lot, its impact is small and perhaps obscure, but it can be significant. Just like you, your life, your experiences, your actions, and your existence have an important and meaningful impact upon the world. One person, one gesture, one action can make all the difference. Be the difference.

Remember as you walk through your day it's the small things that have the greatest impact. A smile, a kind word, forming a new habit or an intentional moment of mindfulness. These small, conscious intentions can have the greatest rewards. Take time to savor the smallest of joys, let us appreciate the beauty of life.

My grandchildren have given me a fresh perspective on the depth of joy found in the little things. A three-year-old delights in the simplest of things—a rock, a bug, or smelling a dandelion. It is all fresh and exciting. I cherish the squeals of discovery and reacquaint myself with life's simplest of treasures.

"Doing the little things can make a big difference." -YOGI BERRA-

Cassie Moor

EBB AND FLOW

The ever-changing tides of life are impossible to avoid. Waves will crash upon our lives, peaks and valleys are inevitable. Life is a messy journey, with twists and turns and unexpected delays. We, as humans, continually fight our valleys. We do not like our lows; it is uncomfortable. Our society fights this notion as well, supporting the idea of staying on top and being the best at our game.

When we accept the valleys with the realization that the lows are part of life experiences, we stay grounded in the knowledge that it is only temporary. We can be grateful for the difficult times, acknowledging the blessings in the smallest of victories. Life is full of surprises and opportunities, and it's essential to be open to them.

If we observe the present moment, even if it hurts or is uncomfortable, we open the mind to learning, growing, and relieving the anxiety of the temporary lows. Sit within the silence of the valleys; there are hidden treasures within.

"One sees great things from the valley; only small things from the peaks."
-GILBERT K. CHESTERTON-

Cassie Moor

SOUL

I would be amiss if I did not speak to the influence of water upon my soul and spirit. I am radically aware and connected to God and spirit when I am near or in water. I love the feel of water as I glide down in its depths, feeling my body strong and buoyant.

I am intrinsically drawn towards water. One of my first memories as a toddler was standing on the shores of a lake, water lapping at my feet. It was pure LOVE.

I feel my best and most optimal near water. For me, water is healing and transformative. I feel balanced in my mind, body, and soul. It is my salvation and reset. I have clear thoughts, increased innovation, and insight.

I associate blue water with calm, openness, depth, and wisdom. I have a general overall sense of satisfaction. It grounds me in the present faster than anything else. I know instinctively that being near water plays a fundamental role in my life. It speaks to my intuition in a genuinely authentic way. I am myself.

"I believe in God, only I spell it Nature." -FRANK LLOYD WRIGHT-

ABOUT THE AUTHOR

Cassie is an interactive speech coach, a distinguished toastmaster, an artist, writer, and photographer. In her role as an executive speech coach, she has trained numerous senior professionals at all levels of communication expertise. Her performance-based approach helps leadership teams and professionals embody presence and confidence to achieve true influence. Speaking is her passion!

As an artist, she has sold and displayed her works in various locations across the country. Her pieces display an affinity toward waterscapes, which are seen throughout the book. She is passionate about her photography and uses her images to inspire her art. She is an avid traveler, which has led her to the shores of numerous bodies of water, where she finds respite. Her mind, body, and soul are intricately woven into the landscape of water.

CONTACT:
A Manner of Speaking, LLC
cassartist@gmail.com

Printed in the USA
CPSIA information can be obtained
at www.ICGtesting.com
LVHW071021091123
763115LV00063B/995